# *Love* INCORPORATED

## The Business of Doing What You Love

JENNIFER NOEL TAYLOR

Editor: Devon Kimball
Proofreader: Rhonda Collins
Cover design: Jennifer Noel Taylor and Patrick Feld
Back cover Photography: Zen Panda Photography, Banyan
Bed and Breakfast Retreat, Floral Designs Maui, James
"Mac" McMinn, Max Henry, Carl Incerto and Thee Salon
Book Design and Layout: Jennifer Noel Taylor and Patrick Feld
Interior Artwork: Jennifer Taylor and Patrick Feld

ISBN-13: 978-0692598023
ISBN-10: 0692598022

www.LoveIncorporatedTheBook.com
Email: Jennifer@LoveIncorporatedTheBook.com

**Printed by Sunflower Press, Paia, HI**

# ACKNOWLEDGEMENTS

Thank you to Patrick Feld for his amazing graphic design work and guidance on book layout, fonts, and images.

Thank you to my dear friend Devon Kimball for her immense help and insight in writing and editing this book.

Thank you to Richard Gordon, my business partner and close friend, for offering his advice as a best-selling author.

And thank you to the Quantum-Touch community for sharing your light and love with the world.

# I dedicate this book to YOU!

*I hope this book inspires you to follow your Heart and live the life of your dreams.*

# CONTENTS

**INTRODUCTION** ............................................... 1
Why did I write this book?

**I QUIT!** ............................................................ 5

**INSIGHT #1** ..................................................... 23
You are a Spiritual Being in a Human Body

**INSIGHT #2** ..................................................... 41
Follow Your Heart *Always*

**INSIGHT #3** ..................................................... 77
Challenges are an Opportunity for Growth

**INSIGHT #4** ..................................................... 97
Be Authentic

**LOVE** ............................................................... 119

# INTRODUCTION

## Why did I write this book?

Love Incorporated is a guide for anyone that feels *stuck* in an unfulfilling job. If your life feels more like a treadmill than an expression of your passionate heart-centered calling, I totally understand!

I spent years at a soul-crushing job before I finally quit to pursue my true calling. After displaying such courage, I thought, *surely* I would be rewarded with instant success! Right?

*Boy, was I wrong!*

Much to my surprise, things did not flow very well. I certainly did not anticipate the sheer amount of challenges I would face!

Through many setbacks and "learning experiences"

(i.e., mistakes!), I finally discovered how to be success-ful *while* following my Heart.

In this book, I address what really works (and what really doesn't!) when you encounter the *unique* challenges of creating a career doing what you love. And I offer some ways to help you discover your true calling.

Fulfilling your life purpose is the most inspiring "job" you could ever have!

*I hope this book inspires you to follow
your Heart and live the life of your dreams!*

# I QUIT!

*Have the courage to follow*
*your heart and intuition.*

**– Steve Jobs**

# "Are you sure you know what you're doing?"

I was talking with my Mom on the phone and she was very concerned with my recent "career decision" to quit my job.

My Mom had every right to be concerned. I had recently graduated with a Computer Science degree from Cal Poly – a degree my parents paid for! And here I was camping out at the house of a friend (and now business partner) with apparently no plan to seek employment.

Even though my Mom was worried, I felt like I was finally released from prison!

*I'm quitting to pursue my dream of not working here.*

## Cold on the Inside

After graduation, I started my first job as a Software Engineer at a big company in San Diego, California.

For eight hours a day, I lived in a cubicle: a special work-

Does your job leave you *cold*?

space that expertly blocked the view from any window, yet failed to mask even subtle noises from other co-workers.

Not only was I trapped in a cubicle, I could have sworn that *someone* had the responsibility to maintain the office thermostat at freezing temperatures. My cubicle always felt like the inside of a refrigerator.

As if the arctic climate wasn't enough, my boss gave me easy, uninspiring, and tedious work. I programmed software that would talk to databases. I had to test very detailed, mind-numbing code. I felt incredibly bored by this lackluster work.

I have a very distinct memory of attending the company awards ceremony. I watched in awe as an employee received an award for thirty years of service. I was shocked that someone had worked at the *same* company for *thirty years*. When he received his award, I couldn't help but notice that he looked very weary; it seemed like his job had taken an immense toll on his joy for life.

That moment was a wakeup call for me. I felt terrified that I *too* would end up as that same burned out person. I couldn't imagine wasting the best years of my life feeling so lifeless and unfulfilled – just so I could scrape together enough money for rent and food.

I tried to find some relief from my miserable work life by changing companies. After just one year, I quit my job in San Diego and accepted a job in Central California. Over the next four years, I worked for two different companies. Yet, I still felt restless and dissatisfied. I was constantly searching for a better life.

I finally landed a job at my dream location: Maui, Hawaii! But even Maui did not sooth my troubled soul. I was living on Maui, working as a software developer, and making a very nice salary. This was a great life... or so I was told. I tried to put on a happy face, but inside I knew that my Spirit was dying.

Every Sunday evening, this feeling of slow dread would come over me, knowing I had to go back to work on Monday. I constantly suffered from a "case of the Mondays"– a depressing sense of foreboding at the beginning of each work week. Every day I would sit alone in my office and

**Do you have a case of the *Mondays*?**

work on the computer. I felt very lonely, isolated, and extremely unsatisfied.

In the morning, I would actually count the minutes until lunch, eager to leave the office for my one hour of freedom. After lunch, I would constantly fight the temptation to sleep through the afternoon. At 5 PM, I would leave like clockwork, cherishing my few hours of freedom until the next work day.

I felt extremely depressed and had fantasies of quitting, but I had no clue how to make ends meet without a job. I felt trapped. I knew I couldn't endure this existence much longer.

In the midst of this beautiful warm tropical location, I felt *cold inside* and incredibly unfulfilled.

# Finding My True Calling

While living on Maui, I started going to massage school after work. I loved practicing massage, but I didn't feel drawn to create a career as a massage therapist. However, massage school *did* provide some much welcome relief

**Everything responds to *Love*!**

from the painful social isolation I felt at work.

At massage school, we studied various healing modalities, including energy healing. Energy Healers channel "Life Force Energy" (also known as Chi or Prana) to help the client facilitate their own healing. I knew in my heart that Love, in the form of energy healing, had the capacity to create miracles and heal almost anything!

Energy Healing turned out to be my favorite topic. I started to feel the energy coming off of people and seeing auras around people. I spent hours playing with the energy coming from my hands.

*One day, the Universe spoke to me and said that energy healing was my life work.*

I had finally discovered my true calling! Everything was about to change...

Shortly after my epiphany, I felt compelled to attend a lecture about Quantum-Touch. Quantum-Touch is an energy healing modality that works with energy awareness and breathing techniques to help facilitate healing. Richard

Gordon, the Founder of Quantum-Touch, was giving the lecture and offering free healing demonstrations. Although I didn't know it at the time, I had just met the man that would turn my life upside down. I felt incredibly drawn to connect with Richard and learn more.

Soon after the lecture, I attended Richard's Quantum-Touch workshop in Honolulu. I instantly fell in love with the vision of Quantum-Touch. By inspiring people to recognize the value of their Love, we could create a much more joyful world. I felt incredibly excited!

After the workshop, I received *yet another* very clear message from the Universe.

*My next step was to become involved with Quantum-Touch.*

# A Leap of Faith

A few short weeks later, I quit my job and bought a one way ticket to Santa Cruz, California: the headquarters of Quantum-Touch. I spent all of my time hanging out with Richard. I had no idea where this would lead... But I had finally taken a *Leap of Faith* and followed my heart. I felt incredibly happy!

**Sometimes your only available transportation is a** leap of faith.

– Margaret Shepard

When I arrived in Santa Cruz, Quantum-Touch was completely failing as a business. Richard had been traveling the world, speaking, and teaching workshops. He decided to take a much needed break from travel, and unfortunately, the revenue in the company fell to almost zero.

Not long after Richard stopped traveling, the then CEO of Quantum-Touch called me and said, "I need to get a real job." She wanted to quit. I could fully understand the need to jump off a sinking ship. She asked if I would like to take over as CEO and I said, "Sure!"

Little did I know what I was saying yes to! I had no background in customer service, no training in accounting, and basically no experience running a business. And yet, I was incredibly excited about my new role with Quantum-Touch!

> *Working hard for something we don't care about is called stress; working hard for something we love is called passion.*
>
> **– Simon Sinek**

# Am I There Yet?

After taking a huge *Leap of Faith* and following my heart, I thought I would be instantly rewarded for my courage! Obviously, I deserved ease, grace, and an abundance of money! Right?

Boy, was I wrong! Rather than enjoying the smooth, successful career I had anticipated, I was dealing with what seemed like an incredible amount of drama and stress! Under my new role as "CEO", Quantum-Touch experienced financial hardship, employee drama, vendors who made promises but didn't produce, an employee lawsuit, an international lawsuit, and the list goes on... Quantum-Touch was (and still continues to be) my greatest teacher!

*When the student is ready, the teacher will appear.*

**- Buddha**

Now 13 years later, the state of the business has dramatically improved. There is virtually no drama. Our vendors do what they say they will, our employees get along well, and we are expanding gracefully all over the world!

**Do what you Love...**
**Create a more loving world.**

The drama and financial woes I initially experienced with Quantum-Touch prompted me to seek a *lot* of help. I attended numerous workshops and I spent years working intensely with a business consultant. I was always reading business books and studying successful businesses at length.

After years of study, trial and error, and self-reflection, I realized that all of my work kept leading me back to the *same core truths* over and over again.

Everything I discovered can be summarized by the *Four Key Insights* that make up this book.

These Insights are a guide to creating a career doing what you love. You don't need to sacrifice your passion, Spirit, love, or integrity to have an abundant business.

And in fact, doing what you love is actually instrumental to creating success in business (and in life!)

*Imagine...*
*If more people did what they love, how*
*much more joyful the world would be.*

*The*
# FOUR INSIGHTS

## INSIGHT #1
### YOU ARE A SPIRITUAL BEING IN A HUMAN BODY

## INSIGHT #2
### FOLLOW YOUR HEART *ALWAYS*

## INSIGHT #3
### CHALLENGES ARE AN OPPORTUNITY FOR GROWTH

## INSIGHT #4
### BE AUTHENTIC

# INSIGHT #1

## You are a Spiritual Being In a Human Body

*Begin to See Yourself as a
Soul with a Body rather than a
Body with a Soul.*

**– Wayne Dyer**

# God is Waiting for You

*You are a spiritual being in a human body.* This concept is quite an assumption about the nature of reality! If you are a spiritual being, this means that there is a part of you – the part I'm calling your Spirit – that is eternal and continues to exist when your physical body dies.

We have no "proof" that life exists beyond our physical death. Many scientists strive to create a rational, logical, or mathematical model of the universe. But even top doctors, physicists, and scientists frequently come up against mysteries that cannot be explained rationally.

Unexplained phenomena suggest that our reality may not be *fully governed* by reason! Even Werner Heisenberg, the father of Quantum Physics, questioned the agnostic perspective of science, "The first gulp from the glass of natural sciences will make you an atheist but at the bottom of the glass, God is waiting for you."

The fabric of the Universe *mysteriously* extends beyond our perception of physical matter into the realm of the Divine.

You are more than the individual elements that make up your body; you are Spirit incarnate. Your Spirit is a spark of the Universe or, as some may call it, a spark of God. If the essence of God is Love, then ultimately, *you are a spark of Infinite Love*.

To say that we are spiritual beings having a human experience, implies that there is a connection between Spirit and matter. This connection, however, is one of the great *mysteries* of the Universe. Philosophers, scientists, mathematicians, and even computer scientists, puzzle over the problem of explaining how beliefs, thoughts, and feelings are related to physical states. This conundrum even has a name: the *mind-body problem*.

I believe that the *Heart* is the mysterious force that links the mind and body. The heart is so much more than a physical organ that provides oxygen to the body. The **"Heart"** is also the embodiment of your thoughts, emotions, and ultimately your beliefs.

*The Heart is the interface between the*
*Spirit, the Universe, and the body!*

Because we are Spiritual beings (in a Human Body), the reality is, at its essence, composed of Spirit that mysteriously interacts with matter. In this Insight, I explore how your health, your relationships, your finances, and all of your life circumstances are actually *messages* from the Universe that reflect the *state of your Heart!*

# Your Body is a Reflection of Your Heart

## Can We Separate Body and Spirit?

Western medicine is built on the premise that the body is separate from the mind, Heart, or Spirit. Doctors use an analytical approach when treating patients – based on the belief that the body is governed by scientific laws.

*But does this perspective always work?*

Let's look at the traditional approach to working with depression...

Over the past two decades, the use of antidepressants has skyrocketed. One in ten Americans now takes an antide-

# Is the Body *Rational*?

pressant medication. Among women in their 40s and 50s, this figure is one in four.

Depression is often viewed simply as a chemical imbalance. Antidepressant medication works by increasing the amount of the neurotransmitter serotonin in the brain. Scientists believe that serotonin is responsible for maintaining mood balance, and that a deficit of serotonin leads to depression.

From this perspective, mood can be changed by altering the chemistry of the body. By using medication, we operate from the assumption that our emotions are a byproduct of the chemical reactions in the body. So, if you control the chemicals in the body, you can control your health and emotions. However, this philosophy may not adequately reflect the true nature of depression nor help everyone achieve a "cure."

The use of medications implies that the patient can not alter their body chemistry *on their own*. This *assumption* may not be entirely accurate, given that the effects of antidepressants (and all drugs actually) seem to contain an element of unpredictability!

# *What* causes the "poop-out" effect?

Most doctors acknowledge that the body develops tolerance for medication over time. While antidepressants may work for a longer period of time in certain individuals, it is likely that everyone will experience diminishing returns.

Doctors have even coined the phrase *"poop-out" effect* to describe the tendency of antidepressants to become less effective over time. Patients simply know this effect as the *scary period* when their antidepressants – once able to quell their sadness – suddenly stop working.

The law of diminishing returns applies not only to anti-depressants, but also to *nearly every drug*. And this "poop out" effect is an enigma; *doctors do not fully understand why medication tends to become less effective over time.*

The "poop out" effect is just one example of the many mysteries doctors encounter when treating the human body. We all have heard stories about patients who "defy the odds" and overcome their disease, even in the midst of a dire prognosis. Doctors often encounter situations where the human body *fails to conform* to rigid scientific principles.

*So what is really going on?*

## Integrating the Heart and the Body

The mysteries of the human body are prompting many people to explore a holistic approach to healthcare. The integration between body, mind, and Spirit is becoming more mainstream than ever before. Even doctors are starting to acknowledge the impact that emotions have on the health of the body.

Your emotions are incredibly powerful. Everyone who has ever felt "heartbroken" knows how intensely painful heartbreak can be. Extreme sadness can actually cause the chest to ache with symptoms similar to a heart attack. And we all know how wonderful joy can feel! Extreme joy can feel like you are bursting at the seams with love; you feel incredibly lighthearted. Intense feelings of happiness can even lessen physical pain.

Doctors are beginning to acknowledge that stress plays a critical role in the body's capacity to heal. For example, some patients experience "White Coat Hypertension." Oftentimes, blood pressure spikes at a doctor's office due to the stress of visiting the doctor! We are starting to realize that emotions can control physical responses, such as blood pressure, that were *previously* believed to be involuntary.

Your emotions are just part of the mind–body equation. Your emotions are also intertwined with your thoughts – a thought can give rise to a feeling, and a feeling can give rise to a thought. Thoughts and feelings both originate from your *underlying beliefs*, which are often unconscious.

# The Power of Your *Heart*

The essence of the mind–body (or Spirit–body!) connection is your *Heart*: the embodiment of your emotions, thoughts, and ultimately your underlying beliefs. I believe that your feelings do much more than just influence your health. *Your health is actually a reflection of the state of your Heart.*

With depression, the Heart feels heavy and burdened. Depression is a message from your Heart that something is not working in your life. So, taking a medication does not address the underlying problem. Medication merely *covers up* the underlying cause for a period of time.

Although medication may work temporarily, ultimately, *you cannot hide from your Heart.* The Heart is incredibly powerful, innocent, and honest. If you are depressed, the underlying heartache must be addressed for the Heart and body to heal.

The *state* of your Heart – the quality of your thoughts, feelings, and beliefs – determine what kind of chemicals are released into your body. Your body is a reflection of your Heart, not the other way around.

*You can't hide the truth from the Heart for long.*

**Remember Boy, money can't buy happiness but it can sure buy a lot of *antidepressants!***

Medications stop working because, ultimately, your Heart is asking you to face your truth. Although frustrating to doctors, the mysteries of the body are actually a testament to the power of the Heart!

# Your Reality is a Reflection of Your Heart

Your Heart not only plays a powerful role in your spiritual, emotional, and physical health, it is also instrumental in the manifestation of your life circumstances.

Have you ever noticed that life flows better when you are happy? And when you are unhappy, everything seems to go wrong...

The notion that you influence your outer reality is even supported by Quantum Physics! Physics is the natural science that involves the study of matter and its motion through space and time. Quantum Physics – the basis of modern Physics – explains the nature and behavior of matter and energy on the level of very small particles (atoms and subatomic particles).

Werner Heisenberg, one of the key pioneers in Quantum Physics, proposed that precise, simultaneous measurement of two complementary values (such as the position and momentum) of a subatomic particle – is impossible.

Simultaneous measurement of complementary values is inescapably flawed; the more precisely one value is measured, the more flawed will be the measurement of the other value. This theory became known as the *uncertainty principle*.

A particle cannot be assumed to have specific properties, or even to exist, until it is measured. In short, *objective reality does not exist*.

This notion that the universe is governed by "probability", prompted Albert Einstein's famous quote:

> *God does not play dice with the Universe.*

Einstein was very distressed about this *apparent* randomness in nature. He was unhappy with the notion that the Universe could be governed by probability- the fundamental premise of Quantum Theory!

Like many scientists, he felt that the Universe *should* evolve according to deterministic laws. How can you predict the future, when you cannot precisely measure both the positions and the speeds of particles at the present time?

Quantum Theory suggests that the world changes simply by observing it. Physical matter assumes a definite state only when perceived.

The true reality is in essence a realm of possibilities – a realm of vibrating energy. Matter does not exist unless you perceive it! The world takes form because you have the power to create patterns of energy from the realm of possibilities.

*The physicists are coming to the same
conclusion that the mystics had – that it
is just the VIBRATION from which
everything came into being.*

**– Dr. Pillai**

Your emotions, your beliefs, and your thoughts *create* the circumstances in your life. The people in your life, your surroundings, your way of life, and your health are all a *reflection* of your Heart. The world is literally your mirror!

The origin of matter is really just infinite Love, reflecting the *state of your Heart* back to you.

*The Reality is actually composed of Love
cleverly disguised as matter.*

## You Are Powerful

As a Spiritual Being having a human experience, your world is a reflection of the state of your Heart. This means that you have the power to create your reality and change your life as well!

Rather than giving your power away to outside circumstances such as people, situations, health issues, or medications, *you can change yourself.* You can have a change of Heart. When you change, your circumstances will transform to reflect the new you.

*You really do have the power to create a life doing what you love!*

# INSIGHT #2

## Follow Your Heart *Always*

*You can fail at what you don't want, so you might as well take a chance on doing what you love.*

*- Jim Carrey*

# Why Am I Here?

All of us at some point or another have probably questioned, "Why am I Here?" Although it may not always be obvious, you have a very specific and unique mission in life: your spiritual purpose.

Your Heart hears the messages from the Universe and you are constantly receiving Guidance to help you align with your true calling.

If you are not following your Guidance, you may feel that doors are closing around you. You may feel lost or disconnected and even *sense* that you are on the wrong path. You may even experience negative circumstances as a way for the Universe to guide you in a different direction.

If you are "on track" with your purpose, you will feel like your life is flowing. There is a feeling of Magic when you are following your Heart: doors will open almost magically, unanticipated miracles will happen, and you will feel very alive.

Your Heart is your compass that points you in the direction of your life purpose.

*There is no greater gift you can give or receive than to honor your calling. It is why you were born. And how you become most truly alive.*

**– Oprah Winfrey**

As you align with your Guidance, you will start to experience moments of incredible magic and joy. Yet it's not always easy to lead with the Heart. If everyone was truly following their Guidance, I believe we would experience a much more joyful world!

Why can it be so challenging to follow your Heart?

- ✓ You may have trouble hearing what your Heart actually has to say.

- ✓ You may have been hearing your Guidance for quite a while but you have resistance to actually taking action.

In this Insight, I describe some ways you can open your Heart and hear the messages from the Universe. And,

Your Heart is your *Compass.*

I show you some ways to overcome any resistance you might feel to *actually* following Guidance – once you are tuned in!

# How to Hear Your Guidance

*I have a plan... do you trust me?*

**– The Universe**

Before you can follow your Heart, you need to figure out what you Heart is actually trying to say! Sometimes you may not even hear what your Guidance is telling you at all.

Here are some tips to help you tune into what your Heart is really saying. These tips are just a starting point... I hope you discover your own unique techniques that work for you!

## Tip #1: Meditate on the Heart

Meditating on the Heart is a wonderful way to open up a dialogue with the Universe and hear your Guidance loud and clear! Here is a very easy technique you can use to meditate on the Heart:

*Create an environment where you are free from distractions and noise. Nature is a great setting for a Heart meditation! Get in a comfortable position, such as lying down. Now, once you're comfortable and free of distractions, start paying attention to your breath. Bring all of your awareness to your Heart as you inhale and exhale. Set the intent to receive messages regarding your life path or next step in that direction. You may receive messages in different ways depending on your level of sensitivity and your unique way to perceive.*

As you meditate on the Heart over time, your sensitivity will increase and you will hear your Guidance more clearly.

When the Universe speaks to you, it's probably *not* going to be in a loud booming voice that can be heard at your neighbor's house! (I personally haven't had any experiences with loud booming voices from the heavens.)

Here are a few ways you may receive messages from the Universe:

✓ You may actually hear a voice but it will be more like the *still small voice* of the heart.

# Typically, the still small voice of the Heart is more *subtle* than this!

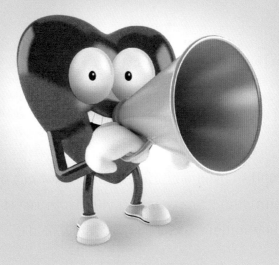

✓ You may feel an intense sense of joy when you contemplate going a certain direction.

✓ You may receive an intuitive hunch about taking a certain step.

✓ You may receive pictures or visual mental images.

✓ You may just get a sense of "knowing" what your truth is.

Just spending a few minutes each day connecting with the Heart is very effective for unveiling your true calling or even just providing you with the next step on your path.

## Tip #2: Explore Your Imagination

*Imagination is More Important than Knowledge*

**– Albert Einstein**

Imagine yourself in a fantasy world where money doesn't exist and you have no responsibilities. What would you do? Suspend all practicality and fear in your mind and delve into your ideal scene.

If you allow yourself to go into your imagination and create your ideal world, you will discover what *truly* brings you joy. You will eventually reconnect with your Love.

Here is another way to tap into your life purpose: if you have an endless supply of money to spend, what would you do? Would you start a business? Would you travel and write a book? Would you join the circus?

Oftentimes, our fear prevents us from connecting with

what we really love. Your imagination is an amazing tool because you can suspend all fear and judgement and just tune into your Heart.

## Tip #3: Create an Environment that You Love

Has your home or office become filled to the brim with objects that are weighing down your Spirit? Do you have stuff around you that triggers sad memories or even things that you *just feel neutral* about? Do you have a lot of things you don't use?

If so, it's time to focus on creating an environment that you love!

Everything carries energy, even physical objects.

If you still feel grief over a previous partner, for example, and yet you still have a closet full of their stuff – this closet is a trigger for negativity. It's time to let it go!

*Only keep what you love. Surround
yourself with an environment that creates joy!*

In the process of eliminating the clutter, you will discover what you truly love. You will find it so much easier to hear your Guidance, when your environment is *only* filled with objects that open your Heart.

You may also find that you save money in the process of cleaning out the clutter. What if you could eliminate your storage unit, or cut back on your housing costs? Or

*It's really hard to focus on what you love when you are distracted by things you do not love!*

maybe you will spend less money buying duplicate copies of things you can't find!

As you clean out the clutter, you will have more appreciation for what you do have. And with your newfound gratitude, you may discover that you are only tempted to buy things you love, rather than items you somewhat like.

*Imagine how much money you could save if you only buy what you absolutely love!*

## Tip #4: Surround Yourself with People that You Love

Surround yourself with people who are supportive of your dreams and love who you are. Let go of the people who disrespect you, put you down, or drain your energy. Eliminating negative people in your life is very important to opening your Heart. You will create space for more people that you absolutely adore and love.

Now, what if you cannot eliminate someone from your life such as a family member or co-worker?

The next best thing is to give energy only to the positive interactions with that person. For example, let's say your spouse is gossiping about a co-worker and the conversation is turning negative and draining you of energy. You can choose to either join in the gossip or you can refocus the conversation on a more positive topic.

You always have the *power to redirect the energy* into a positive place.

## Surround Yourself with Love!

# Tip #5: Eat a Diet that Opens Your Heart

There are many perspectives on diet, but we all know t̲ eating a lot of fruits and vegetables creates a happy body!

Eating junk food tends to create inflammation and pain in the body, making it much harder to connect to your love and your Heart.

Junk food is a very effective way to suppress our emotions. Sugar, alcohol, caffeine, drugs, and heavy foods will force your body to expend its energy processing food rather than feeling emotions.

A lot of emotions typically come up for people who are fasting or eating lightly because their body is spending less energy than normal processing food.

To follow your Heart, it's imperative to be in touch with your emotions so that you can clearly hear the messages from your Guidance! Eating more raw fruits and vegetables will naturally assist you in connecting more fully to your Heart.

## Tip #6: Only Commit to Obligations that Create Joy

It's very easy to become burdened with many obligations that take up massive amounts of your time yet offer no joy. Do you keep certain commitments just because you "should" do them? Do you really resonate with everything you do? I know some commitments (like taxes) are hard to eliminate, but evaluating all of your obligations can really free up your time!

For example, do you really enjoy watching the news or do you feel like you "should" watch the news? Although I sometimes feel pressured to stay up to date on what's happening in the world, I often regret being "informed." I feel much less positive about the world after hearing about another shooting or robbery!

## Creating Space for Love

When you eliminate all of the clutter, negative relation-ships, unhealthy foods, and meaningless obligations from your life, you will have more space to discover what you love! You will have the space and time to focus on what really matters to *YOU!* Your Heart will have the space to unfold. From this place, your Heart will speak to you; you will come to know who you truly are.

It's very easy to become disconnected from who you are in the midst of a life full of burdens that do not feed the soul.

When you connect to surroundings, people, settings, and commitments that *really* create joy, you will get in touch with your true calling.

My desire to be well-informed is currently at odds with *my desire to be happy!*

The still small voice of the Heart is always with you, but it's harder to hear when there's a lot of noise (i.e., distractions) in the way.

*The still small voice of the heart is always with you.*

# Resistance to Following Your Heart

Are you finally listening to your Heart yet still feeling resistance to actually taking action? It's very easy to question the messages you are receiving because following the Heart will typically take you out of your comfort zone!

The Infinite Intelligence of the Universe operates from a vantage point that is broader than any individual perspective. So when you receive Guidance, you may not understand fully *why* you are being guided in a certain direction.

Taking action based on your Guidance requires you to step out in faith rather than have it "all figured out."

Taking a *Leap of Faith* can feel scary, unsafe and impractical among other things – so, it's natural to have resistance to taking action!

However, something amazing happens when you act on faith. When you surrender to your Guidance, you benefit from the Intelligence of the entire Universe – a perspective much broader than any individual.

You will experience the magic of operating from the vantage point of Universal Intelligence.

You will experience circumstances that are not explicable by natural or scientific laws: what I call Miracles!

A miracle can be joyful and *uncomfortable* at the same time

because it will challenge the notion that the Universe behaves in only rational, predictable ways! The lack of predictability inherent in the realm of Miracles is exactly what disturbed Einstein about Quantum Theory.

> *I'd rather have a mind opened by*
> *wonder than one closed by belief.*

As children we believed in magic, fairy tales, and Miracles. As adults, we sometimes lose sight of the wonder and magic in the Universe. But as we follow our Heart and recapture the wonder of a child, we will embrace the magic of life once again.

Even the Bible encourages us to adopt the faith of a child:

> *Truly, I say to you, unless you turn and*
> *become like children, you will never*
> *enter the kingdom of heaven.*

You may hear your Guidance loud and clear and *still* feel resistance to taking action. Resistance is just an opportunity to take a *Leap of Faith*. You can move beyond your comfort zone into the place where *magic happens!*

You can transform resistance into the magic of Divine Flow:

- ✓ Transform the need for logic into the magic of Trust.

- ✓ Transform the desire to "do things your way" into the magic of Surrender.

- ✓ Transform the need to "do the right thing" into the magic of Joy.

- ✓ Transform the pain of letting go into the magic of Creating Space.

## The Magic of Trust
### Overcoming the Need for Logic

When you follow the Heart, the process is not necessarily logical; the progress is *magical*.

We have been conditioned to believe that the route from point A to point B must be linear and must "make sense." So rather than following Guidance, we try to follow logic and "make something happen."

Yet, you will discover that the path of your Heart may be more *miraculous* than logical!

Have you ever noticed that nature tends to operate in spirals and layers? The progression from disease to health is not a straight line. True healing is a spiral process. You continually come back to things you thought you understood to see deeper truths.

For example, many people in the holistic healing field are well aware of the fact that a client may have a "healing crisis." People can experience temporary, yet intense symptoms on deep healing regimes. The body retraces (or goes back) and heals old infections, wounds, injuries, or other imbalances from the past. Healing reactions are an essential feature of all true and deep healing methods.

Following guidance is very similar to the process of deep healing – the Heart is led by an Intelligence our rational minds may not comprehend.

Many times, your Guidance may seem unrelated to your purpose. You may feel this tug at your Heart to let something go, or you may feel guided to connect with someone. You may feel guided to give up something in your diet. (Some things that we consume may actually make it harder to hear our guidance). Or, you may feel guided to connect with a particular person even though it may not make any sense at the time!

If your Heart is leading the way, you will feel *compelled* to follow a certain direction. It will "feel right" to take a certain step even though your practical, rational mind might object.

When I first started working with Quantum-Touch, we did not have any funding (i.e., we were broke!). Shortly after I started working with Quantum-Touch, Richard and I moved to Tucson, Arizona. Being in a new city, I was eager to meet new friends. I felt guided to connect with a woman from our Quantum-Touch community. She met Richard and me for dinner one night and out of the generosity of her heart, she donated some shares of stock to Quantum-Touch. We cashed in on the stock and this donation was an incredible lifesaver to our business. If I had ignored my Guidance and just followed my logic, we would probably be out of business by now!

By putting logic aside and *trusting* the Universe, you create the space for miracles to unfold!

## The Magic of Surrender
*Overcoming the Desire to do things "Your Way"*

When you lead with the Heart, your path may unfold in very

surprising and unexpected ways! The Universe will guide you step by step, but you may not fully understand *why* you are being led in a certain direction. It's so important to trust the process anyway and continue to follow the Heart *always* – not just part of the time!

Trusting the Universe can be *very* challenging because, like me, you probably have your own ideas about how things should be done! But, the Universe has a much broader vantage point than any individual. So following Guidance will help you achieve your heart–felt dreams much more efficiently!

My perspective on following Guidance was *profoundly* changed when I attended a seminar by Doreen Virtue. Doreen Virtue is a very accomplished author and speaker who works with Divine Guidance from the Angelic realm. During the seminar, one of her assistants said that he felt called to start offering intuitive guidance in the form of Angel Readings to clients. He was working as an accountant – a job that was paying the bills but certainly not his passion.

He finally took his *Leap of Faith*, quit his job, and tried to make a living doing Angel Therapy. He thought he was doing the right thing, but he *completely failed* to make a living! Although he went back to his job as an accountant, he still felt compelled to follow his true calling. So… he quit his job for the *second* time and tried again to create a new career doing intuitive work. This time he was incredibly successful and even co-authored a book with Doreen Virtue. What he said next, really struck a chord. When he quit his job for the second time, he actually *followed* his Guidance after he quit.

I was really touched by his story because I finally realized *why* things were not working more smoothly with Quantum-Touch. Although I was pursuing my true calling, I was still trying to do things "my way," rather than following Guidance. I had *mistakenly* assumed that my initial *Leap of Faith* was all that I needed to do!

What I now know is that following the heart is a *constant process of surrender*. If you only follow Guidance part of the way, you may end up back where you started from – at that uninspiring job! It's so important to follow your Heart *always*.

## The Magic of Joy

*Overcoming the Need to "Do the Right Thing"*

I made the mistake many times in business of "trying to do the right thing" according to how other people thought a business *should* be run, rather than following my Guidance.

For example, many people told me that it was important to implement a sales funnel for Quantum-Touch. Basically the idea behind a sales funnel is to create a process that takes customers from the initial contact with the business into a purchase – such as a workshop or product in our case. I was encouraged to create a linear process and monitor each step along the way with different statistics.

To be honest, my Heart was never into working with sales funnels or monitoring customer activity. Yet I believed it was the right thing to do. So I hired different people to create a linear sales process for our business. These employees were great people but it seemed that every attempt they tried was doomed to failure.

I ignored what my Heart was saying and tried to "follow the rules." Ultimately, I ended up spending a lot of money with very little results.

After spending *years* trying to create a successful sales funnel, I finally gave up. Not only were my attempts unsuccessful, I felt absolutely no joy *whatsoever* when contemplating sales funnels! This lack of joy was *clearly* a sign from the Universe that I should be following a different path. I spent years banging my head against the wall and ignoring Guidance because I thought I was "doing the right thing" according to business experts.

When I finally started following Guidance, the path was actually effective! And, I felt a lot of Joy in the process because my Heart felt aligned!

The first set of instructions I received was to focus on cleaning up the clutter in the business. Cleaning up the clutter applied to physical files, files on the computer, cleaning up our website, our email, etc.

Because there was a *lot* of clutter, this process took over a year and a half to do. But, I was drawn to go this route – and sure enough, the business started to improve! In addition to that, we saved money. As I eliminated the clutter, I also stopped spending money to maintain the clutter! For example, we no longer needed to spend money on a storage unit or a massive file server to store all of the data we no longer used!

When I stopped trying to "do the right thing," I discovered that following my Joy was a much more effective "formula" for success. Feeling Joy around a certain path is actually Guidance from the Universe that you are on the right track. Feeling a lack of Joy is usually indicative that you are hitting a wall and you are not on the right path.

## The Magic of Space
### Overcoming the Pain of Letting Go

Sometimes you may feel guided to let something go. Letting go can be painful, challenging and very difficult.

Perhaps a relationship is no longer in your highest good,

or it's time to give up an addiction, or you are being guided to move somewhere.

Although it can be very painful to let something go, the Universe sees things from a vantage point that you do not see. A relationship, for example, may be holding you back from meeting the love of your life. Or, you may feel guided to move. Even though giving up your house may be quite a loss, you may discover that your new location is your *true home*.

Back in 2008, Quantum-Touch had a beautiful office in San Luis Obispo, California. We had seven employees and I was excited that the business was finally reaching a point where I did not have to be involved in the day to day operations! I had just appointed a manager for the office, and I was inspired to move on to more creative projects.

But, in the fourth quarter of 2008, the United States economy took a nosedive. I was distraught. Our revenue dropped by 40% within a matter of weeks. It became very clear that I needed to take action… *fast!* We were in immediate danger of going out of business!

I was very sad to realize that we could no longer afford our beautiful office and that I would also need to layoff several employees. The remaining employees and I all started working from home. I spent a lot of time grieving these sudden changes; I just lost my employees, the office, and I deeply missed connecting with everyone in person on a daily basis.

Losing our central office and employees forced me to develop an infrastructure where people could work remotely. Although I had a lot of resistance to the changes, our new business model provided the opportunity for me to learn how to stay connected with employees and serve our customers without a central office. This new model created the space for us to grow internationally.

We used to be a United States based company only. Now we have liaisons in China, Netherlands, France, Brazil, Japan and more. Obviously, it's very challenging for employees from all over the world to come to a central office! So, the work I did to create a new infrastructure paved the way for Quantum-Touch to grow internationally.

When the Universe is asking you to let something go, it can be a blessing in disguise – perhaps even a graduation to the next level! In our case, the remote business model dramatically improved our ability to grow around the world.

## Follow Your Heart... Always

Embracing your true calling is a *constant* practice of listening to your Heart and following the Guidance from the Universe.

You will feel inspired or even compelled to take action when following true Guidance (rather than feeling *obligated* to take action). Feeling very little Joy around a certain action is the Universe's way of showing you that you are off course. A direction won't "feel right" when it is not aligned.

I was surprised to discover that even after I took my *Leap of Faith* to pursue my true calling, I still encountered a lot of drama and stress. I believe that this tension and strain was actually due to the fact that I wasn't listening to my own Guidance. Although initially I followed my Heart, I then wanted to "do things my way."

The Heart will reveal one step at a time. The process unfolds more like a spiral rather than a straight line (much to the objection of the rational mind)!

You may feel guided to let go of certain situations or people. And you may even question your Guidance when it seems that you are being led in a direction that doesn't make much sense. Yet having the faith to follow Guidance outside of your comfort zone is where the magic happens.

*Following the Heart is a Magical Journey of Trust, Surrender, Joy, and Letting Go.*

Following the Heart is a
Magical Journey!

# INSIGHT #3

## Challenges are an Opportunity for Growth

*A Smooth Sea Never Made
a Skilled Sailor*

# Love Notes from the Universe

Even after you have taken that *Leap of Faith* to follow your Heart and pursue your dreams... the Universe will *continue* to guide you to make things even better (i.e., You will encounter challenges)!

**Challenges are**
*Love Notes from the Universe!*

Challenges are "love notes" from the Universe. The Universe is providing you with a *course correction* – an opportunity to make a change and improve your life.

Course corrections are not that much fun at all! It can be very tempting to view a challenge as *just* another inconvenient fire to put out. Or, you can view challenges as opportunities to become more fully aligned with your true calling.

# Financial Challenges

If you find yourself in a financial bind, it's easy to feel like a victim to your circumstances. It's easy to think, "So I followed my heart and I still can't pay the bills, so much for contributing to the world! I might as well go back and get a 'real job.'" Ha! I've had this thought many, many times! If money is tight, the Universe is asking you to assess your relationship with money:

     ✓ Is your Heart aligned with how you spend money?

     ✓ Is your Heart aligned with how you earn money?

     ✓ Is your Heart aligned with the *concept* of abundance?

# Is Your Heart Aligned with How You Spend Money?

If you are spending more money than you are earning, it may mean that you are putting energy into areas that are no longer serving you on your true spiritual path. This challenge may be an opportunity to evaluate everywhere you spend money and assess whether or not your expenses are in alignment with your truth!

Are you really investing money into only what you love or do you have expenses that weigh you down?

I used to own a house on Kauai, Hawaii. Well actually I didn't own it; the bank owned it! I was making large monthly mortgage payments and the house required constant maintenance. Hawaii may be a dream location but the tropical climate is really rough on houses. I was always spending money and time doing yard work, repairs, and cleaning. On top of that, the house was worth much less than the price I paid for it!

As much as I wanted to own a home, this situation was

more of a burden than a joy. So, I walked away from the house. I felt really sad to let the house go. But, now I rent a place that is smaller, easier to maintain, just as beautiful, and much less expensive. Simplifying my housing situation relieved the financial pressure to meet a mortgage payment. And the landlord (not me!), is responsible for maintenance. What a relief! Letting go of the house, although initially painful, significantly freed up my time and energy!

*Is every expense truly an investment in what you love?*

If your business is in a financial bind, it may be time to evaluate whether or not every expense (or investment) brings you Joy. (OK, there may be *one* exception to this concept: paying taxes! Avoiding drama with the government does provide *some* joy, perhaps.)

If you have employees, does every employee feel aligned with you? Sometimes an employee may simply not be a match for your company, so the Universe is trying to guide both you and your employee in a different direction. And, it's sad but true that a financial pinch may be the only way the Universe can prompt you to actually take action.

Back in 2014, I had some amazing employees working for me, but Quantum-Touch was definitely in a financial bind. It turned out that one of our employees didn't feel fully aligned with working for us. After processing our feelings together about her job, she decided it was in the highest good to leave the company and pursue a different path. Without the financial pressure, we would never have come to this conclusion. In the end, both she and the company are much happier. And she still remains a dear friend to this day.

## Is Your Heart Aligned With How You Earn Money?

If your Heart is not fully aligned with *how* you earn money, it can be very hard to create financial abundance. Even if you *are* pursuing your true calling, you *still* may struggle with a lack of income. You may be offering the most heartfelt, highest quality product or service; but, if you

lack confidence in what you are offering, your customers will pick up on your feelings.

*Your customers will feel your insecurity.*

Sometimes low quality products do really well *just* because there is an energy of confidence behind them. And sometimes potential customers can overlook an extremely *valuable* product (or service) when it is surrounded by an energy of fear or doubt.

Lacking confidence in your product or service will actually

*create* more evidence to support your insecurity through lagging sales.

At Quantum-Touch, we were offering a series of workshops and DVD's/CD's created by one of our top instructors in our company. When he left the company to focus on his own business, my confidence level in the products started to wane and eventually sales dropped almost to zero. The products themselves received great reviews, but I personally felt uncomfortable promoting the products after he left. Sales dropped significantly, and eventually we stopped carrying the products. I believe that my dwindling confidence in the material really created a drop in sales.

When you are following your true calling, have faith that your unique offering will help everyone that the Universe sends your way.

## Is Your Heart Aligned With the Concept of Abundance?

Is your Heart really behind the idea of being financially abundant? The answer to this question may seem to be an obvious "Yes." But I invite you to really explore where your Heart is truly at.

Beliefs around money could very well be creating financial roadblocks. Sometimes when you provide a spiritual service or work based on love, you develop a notion that *real* service depends on doing it for free – that somehow the exchange of money taints your ability to truly serve others.

I see this challenge crop up in my business a lot. Sometimes people offering spiritual healing feel guilty for charging money. I mean, you are just sending the client love, so shouldn't that be free?

I compare this mindset to the concept of selling produce at the grocery store. All of the produce grows for free. You can plant a Papaya tree in your backyard and about eleven months later – voila! You have free Papayas! So why isn't the produce free at the store? You are paying for the labor to grow the fruit, package it up, deliver it to the store, and put it on shelves. In the same way, energy healers, coaches, and other people working with the healing arts get paid for their time, training, and experience.

Have you taken a
"Vow of Poverty?"

Perhaps you have (unconsciously or consciously) taken a vow of poverty: a belief that being poor is more virtuous than being wealthy. Some religious institutions believe that the experience of self-denial allows people to better serve others.

Perhaps this self-denial idea is effective, but I counter that having *more resources* allows you to better serve others.

**86**  LOVE INCORPORATED

When Quantum-Touch has abundant funding, we can actually provide a higher level of service to our community. We can use the funding to create more quality control, a better website, more support for different languages, and more customer service support.

# Relationship Challenges

Both personal and professional relationships are a wonderful opportunity for growth. If you ever feel upset by the behavior of someone else, you have an opportunity to evolve beyond limiting patterns and transform the relationship. I know, it can be annoying to suggest that conflict is a growth opportunity. Sometimes we would just prefer to blame someone else for all of our problems!

# Are You in the Right Relationship?

One of the biggest challenges in relationships is to decide who to actually be in a relationship with!

Sometimes you may simply be working with the wrong person (or people). You can waste a lot of time trying to make a relationship work, when it's just not meant to be.

I had an employee once named Kate* (*name has been changed). She was the root cause of some *major drama* in our company. She spent a lot of time gossiping with employees about other employees. Her meddling not only created a lot of tension, but she masterfully *spun* her tales in such a way that everyone feared being fired!

My office manager was so demoralized that she wanted to quit. And pretty much all of our employees were either depressed or walking on eggshells.

I made several attempts to address her communication style but she stubbornly refused to make any changes.

My only choice then was to fire her. And to top this all off, after I fired her, she filed a lawsuit for "age discrimination."

I pride myself on my ability to create an amazing team of people, so what went wrong? As it turns out, when I hired her, something did not *feel* right.

Although her resume was great on paper, I was not feeling a sense of joy or happiness in her presence – in fact I wanted to run the other way! But, I ignored my Guidance

and hired her anyway. I desperately needed the help and her qualifications looked great.

If a potential employee, friend or partner doesn't *feel* right, it's so important to listen to this Guidance. The Universe is seeing what you may not recognize just yet – that creating a relationship with this person is not in the highest good.

## Feeling Disappointed by Others

Do you feel disappointed by other people? When someone

doesn't follow through on something you thought they should do, it's natural to feel upset. This feeling of disappointment can apply to co-workers, your employees, or even your spouse! And again, you may want to point the finger of blame in their direction, feeling justified that you've been wronged! However, feeling disappointment is actually an opportunity to change how you relate, rather than feel like a victim.

The source of disappointment is usually an expectation of how someone *should* behave. You may expect your spouse to bring you flowers every Friday. You may expect an employee to work extra hours to finish a project. You may expect a good friend to call you several times a week. If you *expect* someone to behave a certain way, you will be disappointed when they don't. And it's guaranteed that people will not meet your expectations. Typically people are *not even aware* that you have certain expectations to begin with!

Your expectations (and feelings of disappointment) actually prevent you from seeing someone as their highest self. If you love everyone for exactly who they are, you give them the space to transform into the truest version of themselves. Everyone wants to feel seen and appreciated for who they are. And people will naturally resist the pressure of trying to live up to expectations. Expecting something will actually chase it away!

Instead of setting expectations, you can work wonders by *negotiating agreements* with other people. In this way, you allow a person to be who they are and then explore the possibility of co-creating together – as long as the agreement is a win-win for everyone!

One time, my business partner and I got into an argument. His apartment rent check had bounced and he wanted to blame me! He was operating under the *assumption* that I was managing his personal bank account! He had an expectation I wasn't even *aware* of. If we would have agreed *in advance* that part of my job was to manage his personal accounting, we certainly could have avoided this argument.

Creating agreements – rather than expecting people to be a certain way – gives everyone the freedom to be themselves, *including you!*

# Unhappy Customers

No one likes to receive a phone call or email from an unhappy customer. And believe it or not, these unhappy customers are really a gift! If you can listen to customer feedback with an open mind, your customers can really help you improve your business.

One day I received an email from Lisa* (*name has been changed). She was very upset about Quantum-Touch in her country.

Quantum-Touch has a program to certify people as *Quantum-Touch Practitioners*. In Lisa's country, many people were claiming that they were certified Quantum-Touch Practitioners when, in fact, they were not! Because she *did* complete all of the requirements to become a Practitioner, this situation rightly seemed very unfair.

At that time, our Quantum-Touch website was only available in English. For people who didn't speak English, there was no way to see the "official" list of Practitioners. So, in non-English speaking countries, people could easily make false claims about their qualifications!

I took her feedback to heart and this prompted me to expand our international program. I hired liaisons for different countries and we started translating our website into multiple languages.

Feedback from customers, especially negative feedback, is another opportunity to make course corrections. You can turn negative feedback into a strategy for becoming more effective at achieving your goals!

## Embrace the Challenges

Financial challenges, relationship challenges, unhappy customers – any and all challenges, can be nerve-wracking and sometimes scary.

Many challenges can pose a threat to your very survival, so the immediate reaction is stress and panic. It takes courage to separate yourself from the emotion and look at the obstacle from the perspective of, "What is the Universe trying to tell me?"

You can use your challenges as opportunities to become even more abundant and even more aligned with your life purpose. Challenges are an opportunity to "course correct" and transform your life into something even better.

Challenges are a
"Course Correction"
from the Universe!

# INSIGHT #4

## Be Authentic

*I had no idea that being your authentic
self could make me as rich as I've
become. If I had, I'd have
done it a lot earlier*

**- Oprah Winfrey**

# Embrace Your Authentic Self

Creating a business doing what you love is ultimately about living a life that is aligned with *who you truly are.* Your *Authentic Self* is the real core of who you are – the expression of who you were created to be.

The *False Self* is who you believe you are *supposed* to be. Perhaps you are suppressing your true self because you are trying to fulfill the expectations of others. Or perhaps your truth contradicts your beliefs about how life *should* be or how you were raised. Going through life as your False Self and ignoring your true gifts, drains your energy and leaves you feeling unfulfilled.

In this insight, I talk about the blocks that prevent you from embracing your Authentic Self and ways to connect with who you truly are.

*I just want you to be fully You!*

**– The Universe**

# What Prevents Us from Being Our Authentic Self?

## Block #1: Our Stories

We all have stories that we tell ourselves; some of them are happy. However, many of our stories are very distressing!

Do any of these negative stories sound familiar?

✓ "I'm a failure."

✓ "I'm unattractive."

✓ "I'm not worthy of love."

✓ "I'll never find my true love."

Our stories tend to stick around because we have highly charged emotions attached to them. The Universe is *always* reflecting your beliefs back to you.

> *Our stories provide profound insights into our beliefs.*

When you feel upset by someone or something that hap-

# What's your story?

pens, you have just gained an insight into a story that is no longer working for you. When you are upset, the Universe is trying to tell you that your story is not aligned with your Authentic Self; the story is a false story about yourself. The story no longer serves your highest good.

Stories are a "double edged" sword. Your stories will attract circumstances that support your story and you will perceive your circumstances to match your story.

The infinite Intelligence of the Universe will continue to bring you scenarios that trigger your story until you release the story. The Universe is inviting you to release a belief that no longer serves you. Releasing a limiting belief is the path to reclaiming your freedom.

The first step to releasing a story, is to *recognize the story that you are telling yourself* when you become emotionally upset. You can release a story when you recognize that you are operating from a pattern, rather than believing that your pattern is your truth. Separating your story from your Authentic Self, is like watching a butterfly finally break free from the cocoon. You have the freedom to evolve beyond your story.

If you are open to the idea that you are operating from a pattern – that the story is NOT who you are – then the negative belief will start to lose its tenacious grip on your life. You can *choose* to let the self-destructive story go. Your life will magically transform to reflect the new you.

You can improve your relationships in business (and life) by recognizing when someone else is operating from a negative story. Instead of taking someone's actions personally, you can step beyond the dysfunctional pattern

**Let go of your stories...
and become the real You!**

and bring resolution to the situation. *Recognizing a story in process can really eliminate a lot of drama!*

For example, one of my employees would become upset when I tried to suggest a different way to do a task. Even if I approached the subject very gently, she would have a hard time with feedback. As a result, I found it *very difficult* to train her and I was feeling frustrated.

After *yet another* unsuccessful attempt to offer feedback

on her work, I decided to talk to her about why she was so emotionally reactive. We both identified that she was interpreting my suggestions as personal criticism rather than a training opportunity. She was reactive because she had a *negative story* she was playing out; she was unable to be present with what was really happening.

After we processed this story, the emotional trigger was disarmed and our work relationship improved. I no longer felt like I was walking on eggshells when I wanted to talk to her about work and she no longer took corrections personally.

# Block #2: Caring About What Other People Think

We all want to be loved, appreciated and cared for. It's natural to suppress who we are – *or even completely change who we are* – so we are accepted by our peers, family, partner, and friends.

Many of us suffer from a split between *who we are* and *who we present* to the world in order to be accepted. If you deny your true calling to seek approval from others, you are creating a disconnection between what your Heart is telling you and the life that you are leading.

*Doing what you love will require you to fully step into your Authentic Self.*

Suppressing your Authentic Self, just to please others, creates a deep sense of dissatisfaction and lack of fulfillment in life.

It's scary to honor your truth when there is the possibility that you will create conflict, anger or rejection. When you stand in your truth, you are pretty much guaranteed to encounter resistance from other people, including naysayers, critics, and people who believe your ideas are crazy! It can be very disconcerting when people criticize you or even express hostility towards your truth.

While running Quantum-Touch, I have certainly had my share of "naysayers" and sometimes even hostile skeptics. I classify Quantum-Touch as an energy healing modality, but skeptics have a different term for our techniques:

*"quackery!"* Even though people in our community have experienced beautiful and sometimes life changing results, energy healing still remains a controversial practice. I have personally been called a "sham" and a "greedy pig." People have made very hostile comments suggesting that we are "only interested in making money" and we "take advantage of vulnerable people desperate for help." I have definitely felt hurt by toxic comments and letters.

In the past, I responded to the cynics with defensive comments of my own. I would get sucked into lengthy exchanges, wasting hours of my time with very little resolution. I learned that it's much better to focus my time and energy on the actual *happy* customers rather than the skeptics. I found that a very polite, "Thank you so much for your feedback" is sufficient for people who just want to vent.

The skeptics and naysayers provide an opportunity to own your truth more deeply. If you can own your truth so fully that you no longer feel defensive by the critics, you will attract less of them!

As you more fully own your truth, you will attract more people who support you!

## Block #3: Self Judgement

Self judgement can be even more damaging than the negativity of others. With self judgement you get pulled down by your *own* critical self-talk.

You can become demoralized by comparing yourself to a certain arbitrary standard such as "beauty," "wealth," or "intelligence." Trying to match certain self-imposed standards *severely* limits your appreciation for your own true gifts.

For example, if you judge yourself against a certain standard of intelligence like your IQ score, you may fail to appreciate your true gift of genius!

The term *genius* is commonly associated with a person who has an exceptional intellectual or creative power or other extraordinary abilities. Einstein is widely regarded as a genius with his renowned scientific body of work. Einstein's theory of relativity and other insights form the foundation of modern physics. Bill Gates, the founder of Microsoft, could be considered a genius. He was perhaps the most visible face of the personal computer revolution in the 1980s and '90s.

Intelligence Quotient (IQ) tests are widely used in education, business, government, and the armed services to assess human intelligence. IQ scores above 140 are generally classified as "Genius." Yet, even Nobel prizewinners in physics – people widely considered as geniuses – have scored below the "genius" level on standardized tests!

Is high "intelligence" necessary to be considered a genius? An IQ test assesses certain intellectual abilities to solve specific problems. But the competency in intellectual reason is just one facet of human potential.

You *are* a genius because you have a unique and extraordinary gift to offer the world. Comparing your gift to a standardized definition of genius will interfere with your unique expression of genius!

> *Everybody is a genius but if you judge a fish*
> *by its ability to climb a tree, it will live its*
> *whole life believing that it is stupid.*
>
> **– Albert Einstein**

"IQ" is a standard that has very little relation to a person's unique ability to profoundly love and inspire others.

Genius can be found in the police officer who prevents a man from taking his life; the officer knew exactly how to give the distressed man hope. Genius can be found in the disabled athlete who completes a triathlon, inspiring millions of people to push beyond their limitations. Genius can be found in the mail carrier who followed his Guidance, and arrived at exactly the right time to help a mom save her baby from choking.

## Our Education System

*Everyone has to take the same exam:*
*please climb that tree.*

If you recognize the genius in others, you will see the genius in yourself. Rather than comparing yourself to certain standards of "intelligence," "beauty," or "wealth," you can embrace your own unique and extraordinary gift.

# What Creates Authenticity?
## Impeccability

Being impeccable with your word is instrumental to success in life and expressing your Authentic Self. Impeccability means doing what you say you will do. This seems like such a simple idea, but it's amazing how many people do not follow through on their commitments – including commitments they make to themselves!

Here are some typical commitments I'm sure we're all familiar with…

> ✓ "I'll send you my expense report on Monday."

> ✓ "I'll go to the gym every day next week."

> ✓ "I'll call you tomorrow."

Maybe you are committed to things that you do not want to do! Your Heart may be telling you that you are on the wrong path. Perhaps the commitments are just obligations that no longer serve you.

Or, do you have too many commitments? It's very easy to underestimate the time it takes to do something and overbook ourselves.

I used to get allergy shots and just dreaded going to get the shots every week. It took time out of my day and it didn't really seem that they were that effective. Although my doctor insisted that allergy shots were worth the time, I just wasn't seeing the benefit. I continued to go out of a sense of obligation.

Since I was frustrated with my allergies and not seeing much help for them, I started to look into eliminating allergies through changing my diet. I stopped eating wheat and dairy and I started eating more raw foods. My allergies started to go away as I improved my diet. So, it turns out, my resistance to getting shots actually led me in a new, better direction!

Sometimes, just keeping track of what you have committed to do may be a stumbling block. But with the technology we have these days, it's incredibly easy to receive a multitude of reminders about all of your obligations!

Upholding commitments creates integrity – both with other people and *with yourself*.

Impeccability is instrumental in creating a *long term* successful business. Businesses without integrity manage to be highly profitable– *initially*. However, customers will eventually discover the true nature of a shady business. Lack of integrity is never sustainable; a foundation built on lies, deceit, or exploitation will eventually crumble. For a business to survive *long term*, it must be built on the stable foundation of integrity.

## Compassion

When you start projecting your *stories* onto people or situations, you disown your Authentic Self. And your projections hurt you just as much as they hurt other people! When you start to make assumptions and create judgements, you

reduce your ability to have compassion for both yourself and others.

One day in a restaurant, a man was drinking a glass of milk. The vegan at the other table started an internal rant in their head: "How can people still be drinking milk... do they not know how bad milk is for you? What about the poor baby calves taken away from their mothers?"

However, the vegan was operating from a very limited perspective. He did not realize that this man was 30 days sober and he was drinking milk instead of alcohol!

You really never know what challenges people are facing in any situation.

> *Have Compassion. Everyone you meet*
> *is fighting a battle you know nothing*
> *about. Be kind. Always.*

One of the worst mistakes you can make in business (and in life) is to make assumptions about a person's motive when faced with a behavior you don't like. Unless you specifically ask questions, you will never know why they behave the way that they do.

Let's say you are dissatisfied with the work quality of several employees. Perhaps they don't care about the company anymore. Perhaps they are upset with the boss. Or perhaps they love their job but they just weren't fully trained. It's easy to jump to the conclusion that an employee has ill intent. However, more often than not, people have loving intentions but lack the training to perform properly.

It may be hard to do, but if you can step back and resist the urge to make assumptions, you will find that you are less likely to takes things personally. Replacing assumptions with compassion, is the path to inner peace.

## Service

When you follow your Heart and pursue your true calling, you also offer your highest service to the world!

> *The meaning of life is to find your gift.*
> *The purpose of life is to give it away.*
>
> **– Pablo Picasso**

When you open your Heart you will feel your connection to the part of you that is eternal; you will feel your connection to the entire Universe.

When you connect fully to your Heart, you will comprehend that love is the fabric of the Universe. You will feel your connection to all of humanity; you will understand that *we truly are all one*. The greatest illusion in this world is the illusion of separation.

When you hurt another, you actually hurt yourself. When you help another, you are actually helping yourself. When you provide the highest service to others, you are providing the highest service to yourself!

We innately want to help others. Service is the pathway to our greatest Joy.

> *Serving others is the most joyful,*
> *fulfilling thing we can do.*

# LOVE

*Love heals everything and love*
*is all there is.*

**– Gary Zukav**

# Love Is All There Is

Matter seems so "real." If we bump into a lamp, it feels like a solid object. But on the Quantum level, the reality is actually a sea of vibration. The reality actually "takes form" when you create it.

The Reality is, at its essence, composed of Vibration (or what I call Spirit) which *mysteriously* interacts with matter. This inexplicable connection between Spirit and matter has stumped many great philosophers for ages! I believe this mysterious connection lies within the Heart.

Your Heart creates the Reality based on the collective energy of your beliefs, thoughts, and feelings. If anger lies in your heart, you will create more to be angry about. When you are connected to your Love, you will create a loving world.

Like a piece of a big Cosmic Jigsaw puzzle, you have a unique purpose that *only* you can do. Your Heart is constantly urging you towards the direction of your true calling.

Living your purpose *requires* you to open your Heart and connect more fully with your Love. Oftentimes you will feel Guided to take a *Leap of Faith* right outside of your comfort zone!

Growing beyond your comfort zone can be very difficult, but also extremely rewarding! Magic happens when you have the faith to follow your Guidance even in the midst of fear and doubt.

When you live your purpose, your life starts to flow! When you follow your Truth, you Heart is filled with joy and you feel "on track."

The Universe is always guiding you to be the highest expression of You!

When you encounter challenges along the way, the Universe is guiding you to more fully align with your Authentic Self. Your life, your surroundings, and the people in your life can *really* be the creation of what *you truly love*.

Living your life with your Heart fully open is your greatest joy. Your Love has the power to profoundly shift your life (and that boring job)!

*A Physician once said, "The Best Medicine for Humans is Love." Someone asked, "What if it doesn't work?" He smiled and said "Increase the dose."*

Imagine if everyone on earth followed their Heart. Every piece of the Cosmic jigsaw puzzle would fall magically into place.

What if the entire planet experienced incredible joy and a state of flow? Everyone could reach their highest potential with their health, finances, relationships, and life overall!

And the Earth would receive the healing she so desperately needs; she too could reach her highest expression.

Experience your greatest joy! Do what you Love and incorporate your Love into everything you do. Your Love is the greatest gift you can ever give – to yourself, to others, and to the planet.

Love is the most powerful, healing force in the Universe.

*Love is all there is!*

SHINE YOUR UNIQUE LIGHT!

DO WHAT YOU LOVE AND...

INCORPORATE YOUR LOVE INTO
EVERYTHING YOU DO!

Printed in Great Britain
by Amazon